Rope Made of Bandages

poems by

Deborah Bayer

Finishing Line Press
Georgetown, Kentucky

Rope Made of Bandages

Copyright © 2023 by Deborah Bayer
ISBN 979-8-88838-176-2 First Edition
All rights reserved under International and Pan-American Copyright Conventions. No part of this book may be reproduced in any manner whatsoever without written permission from the publisher, except in the case of brief quotations embodied in critical articles and reviews.

ACKNOWLEDGMENTS

The Barefoot Review: I'm Still Your Doctor
Cider Press Review: The Heart Doctor: A Ghazal
F.I.N.D.I.N.G.S.: Pucker
healersburden.com/351-2/: Death Rattle
The Healing Muse: Prayer Beads
Juked: White Noise
Hospital Drive: The River
Levee Magazine: In Situ
Mead: The Magazine of Literature & Libations: Window to the Bay
Moonstone Arts Center 2022 Featured Poets Anthology: Mend My Life
The Schuylkill Valley Journal: Bird Neck
Shot Glass Journal: Fertilizer: A Sonnet
The Stillwater Review: Identity
U.S. 1 Worksheets: White Coat Lies

Publisher: Leah Huete de Maines
Editor: Christen Kincaid
Cover Art: Annagrace Kasten
Author Photo: Donna Connor
Cover Design: Elizabeth Maines McCleavy

Order online: www.finishinglinepress.com
also available on amazon.com

Author inquiries and mail orders:
Finishing Line Press
PO Box 1626
Georgetown, Kentucky 40324
USA

Table of Contents

Window to the Bay 1

Pucker 2

I'm Still Your Doctor 3

Wriggle Away 4

The Heart Doctor 6

Bird Neck 7

White Coat Lies 8

Mend My Life 9

How to Grieve 10

In Situ 11

Death Rattle 12

White Noise 14

Electrocardiogram 15

Fertilizer: A Sonnet 16

Tightrope 17

Identity 19

Progress Notes 20

Prayer Beads 21

Thrown From a Window: An Obverse 22

Warning Flags: Sea Isle City, NJ 23

In the Temple of Healing 24

The Indigo Cane 25

Broken Sonnet Corona 26

Sustenance 29

morning song: an acrostic 31

The River 32

In memory of Wayne Cale McAfee
In honor of Charlotte Hewett McAfee

In celebration of the Leap Street poets:
Shelley Cohen
Barbara Daniels
Cole Eubanks
Ben Hyland
Jacalyn Shelley

Window to the Bay

Sometimes I ask my patient, *can you smell it?*
Of course, she can't. Necrosis happens slowly,
a little more each day. There's time to adjust.

My birthday was weeks ago. The flowers are dead.
A clear square vase sits on the kitchen table,
its decay, vegetable. I am no stranger to the foul.

When I examine a blackened toe, I'm always
over-gentle, though the nerves are dead,
as are the muscle, the bone, the fascia.

Look how delicate: a burgundy rose, rimmed
with curls of black. When I touch it, I hear
the sound of tissue paper crinkled around a gift.

I enjoy the flowers, even in death.
My patient is embarrassed by her fetid,
dying appendage. A toe is lost, then

half a foot, then a leg below the knee.
She lies in her hospital bed, so pale she blends
into the bleached sheets. Still she is able

to retract her soul into the part of her body
that's alive. I follow her gaze out the hospital
window. On clear days, I can see the bay.

Pucker

The gods line up
to kiss my left breast.
Divine dimples appear
as I raise my left arm.

A star appears
on my windshield too
when a wayward stone
strikes on the expressway,

loud as a gun's report.
I duck under glass,
wounded again.
Asterisk marks the spot.

I imagine a magical
crystalline fountain
springing out of the ground
and into my chest.

Instead I get
anti-nausea medicines,
a large red syringe
injected so slowly.

My family is grateful
that my car is drivable
and fearful
that I will drive it.

I can still see the road
I tell them,
though another small stone
and I could be shattered.

I'm Still Your Doctor

I happen to be there when you're admitted.
My job is to keep you alive at any cost.
Lucky for you that I have experience
& I'm really good at diagnosing

the opportunistic diseases of AIDS.
So when you have the bad luck
to have a rare pneumonia
& a virus attacking your eyes,

I load you up with several toxins.
to save your vision, to save your life.
You're hesitant about being treated.
I'm sure you won't be when you feel better.

In time I get to see you in the office.
You've gained weight & look healthy.
You wear a beaded & embroidered
white sherwani & matching kufi

over your neat & corn-rowed hair.
You look resplendent. You've come to say
that after long thought & deliberation,
you've decided to stop taking meds

I prescribed so you can pursue
Qur'anic healing under the guidance
of the mullah at your mosque.
My job as your doctor is to let

you make your own decision,
even if I know it means
you'll die. I tell you I disagree
with your choice. I tell you

I support you & that I'm still
your doctor. That was the last
time I saw you, except in the picture
over your obituary in the Press.

Wriggle Away

I fetch a lab coat
to use as a blanket
it hangs

on a metal hook on a coat rack in the foyer

I try to place it
over my son flouncing
the fabric

he'll have none of it

while I stepped away he has become a man
though diminutive

a homunculus

he has his own small lab coat
his name embroidered in red

the pockets are empty
the buttons are all closed
his hair neatly combed

an authority figure
with gravitas

*

he really looks
very little like me
except he's fair
with green eyes

my lab coat pockets are
too full

my stethoscope has to hang on my shoulders
it feels heavy on my neck
I have stains on my collar
and rolled cuffs

my dream son hangs my coat
back on the rack in the hall
and we part ways
these are the last things he does

reads a story

wriggles away

*

his face is a frown
not like the time when, unkempt
hair all askew
he was Albert Einstein
wandering
in Princeton

he played the part of the mad physicist

back then his frown
was a pretense

he was acting the part of an old man
but he moved on the stage with youthful energy

shouting the lines
drawn on his face and hands
like German
cartography

he and I tell stories all night

he is my childhood memory

I am
his

starting gate

The Heart Doctor

A massive MI, myocardial infarction, happens on a plane from London
to LA. The woman doesn't know her distress is a symptom of her heart.

The pastor says, lift up your hearts, and we say, lift them to God.
Everyone else was amazed, but Mary pondered these things in her heart.

My yoga teacher can't decide whether to be anatomic or spiritual.
Sometimes she says sternum, sometimes she says space of the heart.

Green is the color of the fourth chakra. The one where energy spirals
both ways. From the back, from the front, both in and out of the heart.

My patient is very calm, says he won't harm himself. He has a plan.
He has no friends. He has no gun or sword. He's not the King of Hearts.

My mother-in-law gave me a black trunk to use as a hope chest.
I stored the quilt she made for me, a pattern of ribbons and hearts.

Deborah, you can pray and breathe and meditate and chant, give
and receive love, but you can't keep everyone safe in your heart.

Bird Neck

What's my basic unit of currency?
It's not dollars.
Each patient makes a withdrawal.

What's the exchange rate?
It's not Medicare payments.
Each prayer makes a deposit.

Fifteen years since he tested poz.
His first doctor visit with me
is supposed to last seven minutes.

His eyes are already red.
I take in his cornrowed hair,
his hollowed cheeks. My cold hands

on his bird neck feel dismay, but my note
says adenopathy. I haven't felt
those shotty lymph nodes in a long time.

Why am I still doing this?
Each poem I write is an interim
statement, so I can be reconciled.

White Coat Lies

Rain in November deepens depression,
worsens all joint pain. *On a scale of one
to ten it's an eight.* The waiting room
is full of dripping umbrellas.

I walk to the front desk. The waiting
woman sees me. Even my stethoscope
disguise, my averted gaze won't deter her.
She asks for minutes of my time.

I tell her I can't talk now.
I'm with another patient. I fear the request
for a disability letter, an opiate prescription.
She doesn't argue with my authority.

My bright blue computer screen waits
to finish my progress note. I like days
when I keep up. I like days when I'm done
before the building closes, before

the sliding doors lock. After six, no one
can come in, no one can get out, except
by the panic bar door. The security guards
frown, stare at gray video monitors.

I smile at them as I leave.
The asphalt lot looks different in the dark,
gates raised for the night. Open umbrellas
get blown inside out by the wind.

Mend My Life

In the middle of hours, I walk out,
out of the clinic and into the rain.
My nurse's round face

behind the front glass door worries
as I turn right onto Jimmie Leeds,
straight past the Seaview Resort,

down to the White Horse Pike,
east toward Atlantic City. Water
in the marsh crests onto the road.

No one is fishing off the bridges
as Ohio Avenue curves, straightens
to Bally's, with copper windows

dimmed by clouds and fog. Inside
I cross the smoky casino, assaulted
by bells, lights, the thumping music

of Tower of Power, until I get to
the Boardwalk, to the wild gray
ocean, where the wind whips

my hair into my eyes. Pulse racing,
gulls laughing, I stand shivering,
exhilarated, no lifeguard on duty.

How to Grieve

Don't tell your patient how sad
        you are that he stopped
                taking his meds.

Keep your professional face on.
        Tell him there's no use
                in regret. *We need*

to move forward. After he dies,
        don't be surprised at the tears
                that slide down your face

as you comb your hair and get ready to go
        back into the hospital, see other
                patients in the same room

where he died. Healing touch is too much.
        Let your masseuse try hands-off Reiki,
                which also doesn't work.

Let her talk you into Transformational
        Breathing, guided hyperventilation
                that helps somehow.

In Chinese medicine, grief is processed
        through the lungs. Years later,
                hear more clearly

how his mother whispered in your ear
        Thank you for all you did for him
                when you hugged her.

In Situ

Even before I open my eyes, the light in them
is orange, as red buds give way to masses of pollen
and pale new leaves. The changing foliage makes

a filter for sunlight through the glass: amber,
pale green, then emerald. This tree and I have traveled
a score of journeys together; four years since my diagnosis.

Each year, the colors are farther from my window.
Another limb has died. This summer, I'll turn
my attention to the earth. A single yellow blossom

sings to the bumblebee, which attacks;
bee and blossom merge. The flower's stem bends
under the weight of the bee but springs

up again and sways as the bee straight-lines away
as suddenly as it landed. The crimson leaves of autumn
will desert the chokeberry bush, leaving red fruit behind.

The cardinals have their fill, especially the female
with her bright orange beak and gray plumage that
only hints at redness. In winter, I look to the sky.

Comforters of snow and prisons of frozen rain
encase the woods in brilliant fire. Orion's Belt
stands out sharply among the midnight swarms of stars.

Moonlight intensifies the white discoloration of lichen
patches on the bark. The bare branches as unfamiliar
as my own chalk-white skeleton.

Death Rattle

Back when five and dimes
still made black and whites,
I loved the cloudy bubbles

made by pouring soda over
brown-syruped vanilla ice cream.
Today, the ShopRite-brand Dark

Roast is bitter without complexity.
I donate the open-but-full can
to my office. I leave my Blackberry

behind on my white desk calendar
as I rush off after hours.
I blame it on hunger. Someone else's

turkey pot pie is in the toaster oven.
At the ICU family meeting, we talk
favorite stuffings until the latecomers

arrive. Then we ask a man's family how
much they understand before
we recommend taking their father

off the ventilator while keeping him
comfortable. On my way past shops
on Arkansas Avenue, I glance

sideways at the inside of Skechers,
an intense, white fluorescent
island floating in the asphalt night.

Shoeboxes, white with pink lids
like thousands of iced cakes, cover
every wall. I'm looking into a dollhouse

bakery. Black Friday sale signs make
dark silhouettes that block the fairy light.
On the Expressway, a series of bright blue

billboards shout white lettering:
Nice try, Sandy, but we're Jersey strong.
I'm not cheered or encouraged.

Near home, I hear a soft rattling,
like a chain saw in the distance.
So many trees need to be dismembered.

A dry leaf is caught in my wiper blade.
It oscillates in the wind,
sings in a deep register.

White Noise

My red-haired nurse carries a white box
that trails an electrical cord. "I have to
ask your opinion," she says. "Which one

of these settings do you like? Patients are
complaining about the crying kids next
door in Peds." I don't like any of them.

Not the white one, not the ocean. My brain
understands that one sound drowns out
another, but my body doesn't. I feel my gut

twist when the decibels go up. The loudness
is a hissed monotone. I go into the echoing
room where the new machine is installed.

I feel off-balance but I adjust, as I do when
I hear a child crying. I mention the new sound
to the patients. One thinks it's a ventilation fan.

Another doesn't hear anything at all.
I notice the constant exhalation. I take a long
breath in. I'm surprised people need

to drown out the symphony of children. I follow
the quality, tone, cadence, and pitch of the wails.
Why don't others immerse themselves

in these waves? My eardrums vibrate
with the songs of the betrayed. The crying
has benefit. The children are soothed.

The noise won't go on forever even
when it's ratcheting up. It'll come
to a gasping, shuddering end.

Electrocardiogram

Lying on an exam table, pant legs hiked up to reveal my shins, sweater and bra pulled up to reveal six contact points for the sticky pads, I'm here to get a tracing of ink, squiggles to show the electrical activity of my heart. As Nayla attaches the electrodes, I chat to break the silence as I stare up at the ceiling. Chatting is okay now. We're past the awkward meeting stage. She's already given me a flu shot, already established I am a patient today, not a doctor. My gaze is inward until I break the silence. *Back in the 70s,* I say, *I did what you're doing.* What made you want to be a doctor? she asks. *I got bored. I wanted to work with people.* Silence for a moment, then she speaks. Back in my country, I was a gynecologist for 25 years. Here, they said I had to train again. I'm 54. I can't repeat those six years. We have taken opposite paths. She returns to her machine. No talking now. I stare toward the ceiling but I don't see it. Afterward, I pull down my pant legs, my bra, my sweater and sit up. *Thank you,* I say. She smiles over her mask as she closes the door behind her. We are back to pleasantries. *Nice to meet you.* Same here.

Fertilizer: A Sonnet

She plows the furrows, pushes past her wants.
Can she imagine rows and columns, summed
on spreadsheets as the basis for her work?
Or, does she dig down to her ballet class,

dance to Tchaikovsky all in lacy-white tulle
stitched with plastic violets for the waltz?
She isn't graceful, but she moves with joy,
forgets herself, and driven to succeed,

puts gashes in the ground, and the manure
comes with the strain of overtime, and yet,
beneath the stony ground, each seed still sheds
its coat. The rootlets reach for sustenance.

The weak shoots seek the sun, and bidden or
unbidden, here, new blades of palest green.

Tightrope
  for Fran

They will stumble, fall
as they feel their way
in soft-soled shoes.

He is weak, and she's not
strong enough. He fell
in the bathroom after

she lifted him out of bed.
He flubbed the LSAT
despite the prep, despite

straight A's in 4 years
of undergrad. He didn't
feel like himself, then

the diagnosis. The 5-year
plan is gone. She'll finish
her master's. Law school

will wait; there is much
uncertainty. A virus
attacks the brain's white

matter because a virus
killed some white blood
cells. Progressive Multi-

focal Leukoencephalo-
pathy. It's hard to say
if you have it. It's hard

to stand, pivot, shower.
It's easier if you break
the words down.

Medical terms are simple.
If you know what each root
means, you can figure it out.

Leuko- (white)
encephalo- (brain)
pathy (something is wrong)

Identity
    for Alex

Tall enough to get her bag
easily from overhead,
She's in business class,
one of the first to stand.

Her gray jacket and dress
make her feel poised.
The matching opaque
pantyhose are size Q2.

The Mary Jane pumps
have the tiniest of heels.
Chunky jade earrings
balance her aquiline nose.

Her auburn layered bob
flatters her face. She turns,
sees him staring at her from
just behind the curtain

in coach. Makeup hides
her five o'clock shadow.
It's been a long flight,
Philadelphia to Phoenix,

but she loves landing
in the desert at night.
The ground's darkness gives
way to a net of blue stars,

then to white ones near the city.
The man looks away quickly,
but in the few seconds
his eyes lock to hers,

his expression startles her.
When she was a boy,
her mother used to
look at her like that.

Progress Notes

I could easily be overwhelmed
in the Substance Use Clinic.
I saw six people in one afternoon,

and on the outside, I remained calm,
controlled. I don't know what I don't
know. I stayed open, and I received

the unknown. I waited until today
to write my progress notes. My body
and mind need time. Now names

become narratives: Abdul, Deborah,
Ivonne, Olga, Sunny, and Trish.
Some put me at ease. Some put me

on the defensive. Each one needs
a different type of parenting, which
doesn't come easily. Reflection,

deepening come later. There's
nothing to forgive. I sit on my mat
in easy pose, with right leg crossed

over left. Sit up tall with a tremble
in my legs. Energy moving through.
My attention is drawn to small things.

A large black fly buzzes around
my head. The squirrels have stolen
insulation to make their nests.

I am not annoyed, though we are
in conflict, these small ones and I.
To each according to the need.

My job is to allow the spider
in my sink to struggle. She can't get
traction on the smooth white surface.

Prayer Beads

I long to leave the doctor's life behind,
but patients are still pulling at my sleeve.
I head for healing of another kind.

Four days a week I keep a writer's mind
and pray the words and stanzas flow with ease.
I long to leave the doctor's life behind.

The other three are days I run behind
the schedule and try my best to please.
I need a healing that is soft and kind.

My pen moves smoothly over pages lined
in purple ink. I argue my conceits.
I long to leave the doctor's life behind.

I think I know myself, but am I blind?
The writing life is bitter and it's sweet,
a font of healing of another kind.

For years I've held these prayer beads in my mind,
but now it's time to scatter them like seeds.
I long to leave the doctor's life behind,
to head for healing of another kind.

Thrown From a Window: An Obverse
with thanks to Nicole Sealey

Quarantined for more than forty days, *quaranta*
in Italian, we're placed in isolation. We aren't
sequestered, not like carbon. We won't save

the environment nor the bone detached from
its blood flow, dying. The child with sickle
cell has blood trapped in her spleen, dying.

Grim reality hides behind a Latinate
mask. Defenestration is a fancy word
for mob violence. Quarantine is a sequined

evening bag, lying useless. Rain on the roof
drums a rhythm that's not iambic. The meter
is staccato, chaotic, like sequester, all amphi-

brachs, breaking patterns, against the flow,
the wonder, horror of an open window.
The wonder, horror of an open window
brachs, breaking patterns, against the flow,

is staccato, chaotic, like sequester, all amphi-
drums a rhythm that's not iambic. The meter
evening bag, lying useless. Rain on the roof

for mob violence. Quarantine is a sequined
mask. Defenestration is a fancy word
Grim reality hides behind a Latinate

cell has blood trapped in her spleen, dying.
its blood flow, dying. The child with sickle
the environment nor the bone detached from

sequestered, not like carbon. We won't save
in Italian, we're placed in isolation. We aren't
Quarantined for more than forty days, *quaranta*

Does chaos always lead to death?

Warning Flags: Sea Isle City, NJ

Birdsong wakes me, trilled, intricate,
not the simple three-tone tune I hear
at home. Last year's pine needles

are strewn over the ground like rusty
pipes. Roofs peak under intense blue.
I celebrate the lessening of rust

in my joints now that I can walk.
I see a fading ornamental plum
devoid of fragrance, blossoms

brown over a parked white ice truck
(I once thought all block ice came
only from Sea Isle City.)

A red neon Open sign is dim
in the daylight. Two years since
my last radiation treatment of free

radicals. The oncologist told me not
to take vitamin C. It would counteract
his electrons. I took it anyway, hoping

it would soothe burns on my skin.
Despite stones laid over the ground,
despite toxic weed spray marked

with white fluttering warning flags
(they're stamped with green silhouettes
of crossed-out children), some weeds

still emerge: a solitary dandelion
with jagged toothy leaves, clumps
of purple flowers whose name I don't

know. Spring leaves are reddish-brown
until I remember I'm wearing shades.
Without them, the leaves are green.

In the Temple of Healing

When I leave the sea-filled chamber,
the guide gives me a gift, a clean

white handkerchief with two stones
tied in the corner. I untie the knot,

take one of the prisms in my hand. It fits
my left hand true when my fingers close

over the polished surface. I feel a deep
hum. The other rock takes getting used to.

It's the one I keep with me. I bring it
to the clinic in the pocket of my backpack,

nowhere near my cell phone. I fear sharp
edges will mar the screen, or the phone

signal will interfere with the energy.
The surface of the quartz is scratched

and sticky, as if it once bore a price tag.
Soap and water won't smooth it; neither

will alcohol. It doesn't come clean, but
it holds my warmth as it transmits the light,

broken into seven colors. I have two
crystals, an unblemished one at my bedside

and a rough one in my pocket. Do I love
both the same? No, I love one more.

Let the pristine one stay home, protected.
The scarred and clouded one is me.

The Indigo Cane

Rushing to chemo, I missed the last
step to the concrete garage floor, agony
relieved when the bones snapped back
into place. A pale blue icepack sat

on my ankle as I multitasked
at cross purposes: alleviate swelling,
receive toxins. Friends offered
too much sympathy as I limped,

shiny metal indigo cane in hand.
I still had to bear my body weight
with every step. I preferred to be
invisible. Gray, every morning,

the color of my joints. I pushed
through it. I couldn't float that color,
not like the migraines: for a second
or two, the top of my head opened,

and the red ball rose, then re-entered,
throbbed under my fingers, always
the same spot above my right eyebrow.
On a tour bus in Wales, eight years later,

delirious from jet lag, strong shadows
of cars appear as women dancing
on the berm. They remind me
of black cutout shadow puppets.

The bend of the curb forms
the women's shoulders, the grass
is the texture of their hair. They jump,
shimmy, and toss their green curls.

Broken Sonnet Corona

ii.

No workers leave their homes, they're stuck indoors.
In front of Zoom or Skype, they teach their kids
new problems — math and US History,
comparing Covid to the Spanish flu.

I talk to anxious patients on the phone,
assure them that next time they can come in,
we'll catch up on the shots and labs they need.
Right now, they should wash hands and stay inside.

And meanwhile, I'm the only one to stir,
no traffic on the roads as I drive in.
My life has hardly changed, my week's the same
except for envy of those closed within.

My pack of PPE is safely stowed
where no one else will find my mask and shield.

iii.

No one else can find my mask and shield.
I've placed them high above the others' reach
among the textbooks no one ever reads,
the ones they shun, and I no longer need.

I studied long and hard for Board Exams,
but all that time and labor come to naught
when faced with something no one's ever seen.
I'm learning as I go; I've not been taught

how to explain a novel virus to
my patients and my family and friends,
like teaching higher math to my own child,
I have to read at night to stay ahead.

I know the trust that's placed in my white coat.
I never want to let my patients down.

iv.

I never want to let my patients down.
It's well ingrained – *They call me and I go,*
and yet I know the time is coming soon
when I must let another take my place.

A virus led me into what I do.
I loved the patients who had HIV.
Another virus now has changed the world,
a closing bracket to my clinic life.

As bit by bit I dampen down the flow
of energy that burns between our hearts,
I think I'm being kind to move away.
It's me I must protect as ties are cut.

This social distance comes at a good time.
I'd rather skip the awkward long goodbyes.

v.

It's better than an awkward long goodbye.
My boss asks me to cut my hours down.
I'll work one day a week, have time to write,
soldier on and slowly fade away.

Lub dub lub dub my heart says when I place
my stethoscope just at the sternum's edge,
but love's a different language in my head,
a Cadillac-pink streak along the road.

Even if the chassis drags the ground
weighed down by all the loves who call me Doc,
I keep on moving toward a new work dream
to put both heart and mind upon the page.

I'm free of being at their beck and call.
With coffee's help, I set a steady pace.

vi.

With coffee's help, I set a steady pace
in early morning sessions with the pen.
And yet I feel the tug toward my old life.
A colleague calls me for a curbside chat.

I recommend a dose of Fosfomycin
to give his patient with a UTI
then try to dive back into the cool water
of my thoughts, but now that pool is dry.

I count the days until I yield the reins.
I know the nurse practitioner has been hired.
She's smart and caring, though she has her quirks.
Her patients love her too, and so it goes.

I have not come unstuck in time; I'm here.
Like Janus, face both old and new, no fear.

vii.

As Janus faces old and new, no fear,
I move beyond my past to shape the way.
My old wounds are not healed, despite the wealth
of goods on my apothecary shelf.

Like the centaur Chiron I am doomed
to fail to heal myself. Yet, in my quest
I share what I have learned along the path:
immortal and base mortal fused in me.

When Chiron ceased his struggle, sought to die,
he became a star in the night sky.
And now acceptance creeps up on me, too,
I let fresh soldiers raise the medic flag.

With Chiron as the grounding in my art,
I gaze from earth to sky and see the stars.

Sustenance

I love the moving white light
on the baby-blue screen
as if it were my patient.
That's how I dream

about work now, screens
instead of people, light
in wave-particle duality,
frequency and photons.

I'm keeping someone
alive as Vishnu does--
sometimes the Preserver
sometimes the Sustainer.

Like my piano pedal,
I'm trying to prolong
the last sweet notes
of the singing bowl,

green quartz, the color
of the heart chakra, so
the sound resonates
in my chest. I move

fast, but I slow down
to listen. A friend breast-
feeds her baby. Her food
sustains them both.

From my lunchbox, I take
a Ziploc. I see saltines
smeared with peanut butter.
A bite's missing from

one corner; I remember
being hungry. Before sunset,
I see a heart surgeon float
on his back through the sky.

In orange scrubs,
I'm a hospital prisoner.
When I escape to the gym-
cafeteria, the faceless crowd

wears orange, and I don't.
Maybe they're monks, mourning
the losses they've sustained.
I feel them chanting

Om,
Shanti.

morning song: an acrostic

sometimes   i am no longer a doctor
every day i tell that lie as an affirmation
maybe if i say it as if it's already true
i can begin to
reel in the serpentine fish of trauma
every night in dreams   of spring rain
the past comes as white light beams
in streak-free windowpanes
relief from   shouldering   is elusive
eels are less slippery than a chance to rest
may all beings be happy   including me
each day begins with opening   my heart
now there are times when it stays open
to the day   my chestplate drops away

The River

The clinic door clicks behind me—
yes, it's still unlocked.
The smell of fresh water
breathes me to the open window

where I let down my handmade rope
made of bandages knotted together,
and lower myself to the bank
where the reeds grow in the mud.

A reed raft and a reed flute—
both useful in their hollowness.
I sink my toes in the silt,
wade into the blackness.

Craft and current carry me.
The less I struggle,
the more the river takes me
where I want to go.

Rope Made of Bandages is **Deborah Bayer's** first poetry collection. She has spent twenty-eight years caring for HIV patients in the Atlantic City area. Her poems have been widely published in journals and anthologies, and she is working on a memoir about her medical career. Teachers and mentors include Stephen Dunn, Kathleen Graber, Renee Ashley, Cynthia Arrieu-King, and Peter Murphy. She is working on a Certificate of Professional Achievement in Narrative Medicine from Columbia University. Narrative Medicine applies an approach of openness and discovery to artwork, literature, and human relationships. The poems in this book reflect the Narrative Medicine approach: poet as physician, poet as patient, and poet in transition from clinician to retiree. She spent her early years in Brazil and now lives in Galloway Township, NJ with her husband.

www.ingramcontent.com/pod-product-compliance
Lightning Source LLC
Chambersburg PA
CBHW022125090426
42743CB00008B/1004